Contents

Any words appearing in the text in bold, **like this**, are explained in the Glossary.

What is sound?

Sound is what we hear when something makes a noise. This dog is barking. Everyone around it can hear the sounds it makes.

Sometimes you can hear many noises at the same time. The people in this street can hear the sound of cars and people talking.

Making sounds

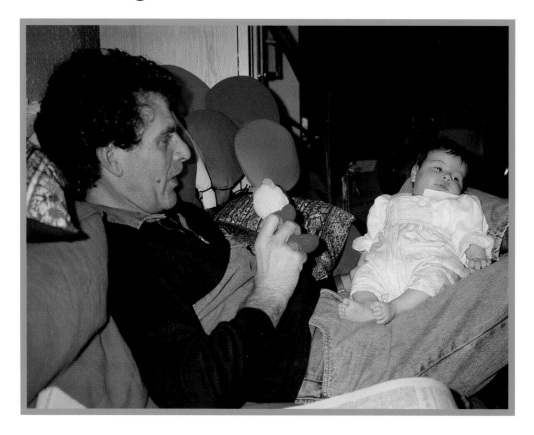

There are many different ways to make sounds. This father is shaking a rattle to make a noise. Banging, scraping and rubbing also make sounds.

These children are making plenty of loud noise! Each child is making sounds in a different way. What is each one doing to make a sound?

Describing sounds

There are many words to describe how a noise sounds. These bells make a 'ding-dong' sound. An alarm clock makes a different kind of ringing noise.

Spanish dancers sometimes use **castanets**. Castanets have two parts. Dancers snap them between their fingers to make a clicking sound.

Loud and soft

If you bang something hard, it will make a loud noise. But if you just tap it, it will make a soft noise.

This cat is purring softly because it is happy. These are some words that describe loud sounds — shout, bang, roar, clatter.

Vibrations in the air

When you **pluck** the string of a guitar, it moves back and forwards very fast. This makes the air around it **vibrate**.

The vibrating air makes the sound. The **vibrations** move through the air like the ripples on a pond.

Ears and hearing

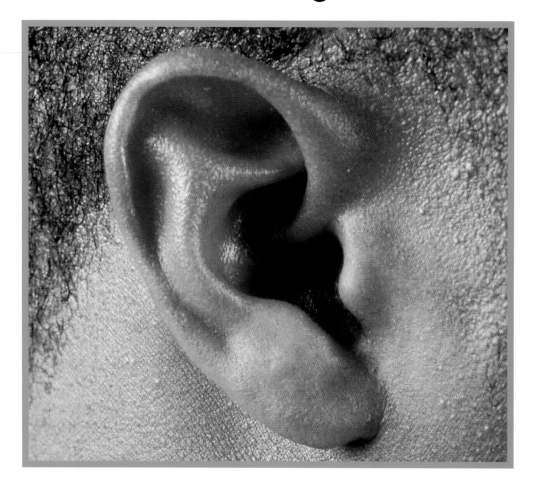

You hear sounds when **vibrations** in the air reach your ears. The vibrating air makes your **eardrums vibrate**. The vibrations pass inside your ears.

If you cover your ears with your hands or with **earmuffs**, you cannot hear so well. This is because less moving air reaches your eardrums.

Talking

People can make sounds and talk because we have **vocal cords** in our throats. As you breathe out, the air makes the cords **vibrate**.

Put your hand on your throat and make a noise. Can you feel the cords vibrating? You make different sounds by moving your lips, tongue and teeth.

Musical sounds

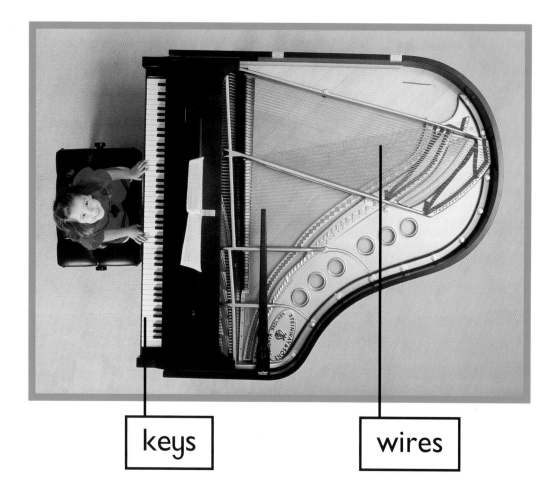

keys

wires

Musical instruments make air **vibrate** in different ways. The piano keys are joined to wires inside the piano. When you move the key, the wire vibrates.

When you blow into a recorder or a trumpet, you make the air inside it vibrate. When you bang a drum, the top vibrates.

High and low

Musical instruments make many
different notes. When you **pluck** a
short violin string, it makes a high note.
A long string makes a low note.

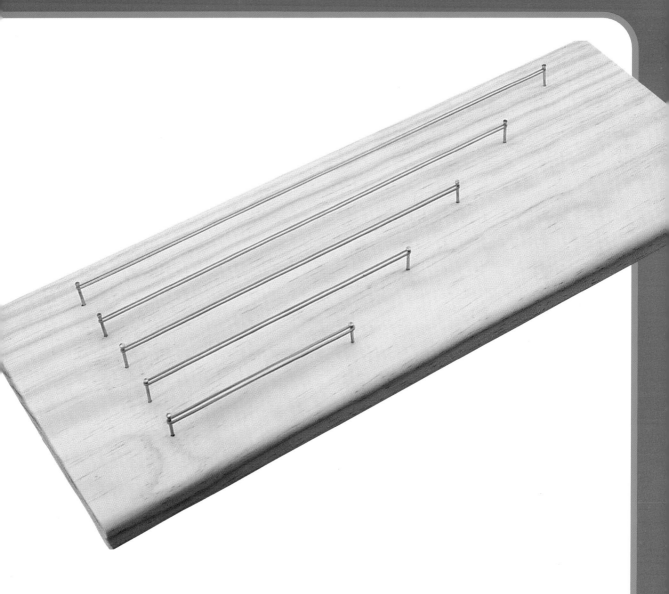

You can make your own instrument using rubber bands stretched between nails. Which rubber band do you think will make the lowest note?

Sound travels

Sounds are louder the closer you are to them. The noise of this aeroplane becomes quieter and fainter as it flies further away.

Pour a fizzy drink and listen. You should be able to hear the bubbles bursting. When you move away from the glass, the sounds no longer reach you.

Hearing but not seeing

What sound are these girls making? Sound can travel around corners. The boy can hear the sound, but he cannot see who is making it.

Sound can travel through wood, water and most other things. The person in the house cannot see who is knocking on the door, but they can hear them.

Where is it coming from?

We have two ears to help us hear where sound is coming from. When you cross the road, you must listen as well as look for traffic.

Turning your head can help you tell the direction of a sound. When you cannot see, you must listen hard for any noises.

Dangerous sound

Very loud noises can **damage** the inside of your ears. If this happens, you may go **deaf**. These men are wearing ear protectors to keep out the sound of drilling.

If you listen to music through headphones, make sure the sound is not too loud. Look after your hearing so that you can enjoy what you hear!

Glossary

castanets two pieces of wood which are clicked together by the fingers

damage hurt or injure

deaf not able to hear

eardrum very thin sheet of skin in your ear

earmuffs things you put over your ears to keep them warm

pluck pull strings with the fingers

vibrate to move a small distance back and forwards very fast

vibrations very fast movements backwards and forwards

vocal cords pieces of skin that vibrate when you speak

Answers

Page 7 – Making sounds

The girl is tapping a drum. The boy on the left is plucking the strings of a guitar. The boy on the right is banging with a hammer.

Page 21 – High and low

The longest rubber band will make the lowest note. This is because the nails it is stretched between are further apart.

Page 24 – Hearing but not seeing

The girls are making a clapping sound with their hands.

Index